. . . *a lot on my mind, Lord*

by
Karl E. Lutze

Published and distributed by Orchard House
Printed by Home Mountain Publishing Co., Inc.
Valparaiso, Indiana

First Edition. First printing October 2005.

Printed by Home Mountain Publishing Co., Inc.,
2102 North Calumet Avenue, Valparaiso, Indiana 46383.
(219) 462-6601.

Library of Congress Control Number (LCCN) 2005934192

ISBN 978-09773511-0-7

ATTENTION CORPORATIONS, UNIVERSITIES, COLLEGES, AND PROFESSIONAL ORGANIZATIONS:
Quantity discounts are available on bulk purchases of this book for educational or gift purposes. For information, please contact Orchard House, PO Box 469, Valparaiso, Indiana 46383.

Acknowledgement

A generous gift from the Reverend John and Eileen Frerking of North Palm Beach Florida, has made possible the publication of this book. The gift is intended as a tribute to the life and ministry shared by the Reverend Leslie Frerking and his wife Katie, remembering their love for our Lord and his people and their years of service to the Southeastern District of the Lutheran Church-Missouri Synod and Ascension Lutheran Church in Charlotte, North Carolina.

I am deeply grateful for my friendship with the Frerkings and for their support of my ministerings.

I am eager also to acknowledge the great assistance my own family members gave me in preparing this book, especially Gail, Hilda, Mark, and Hildegarde and, of course, Katrina whose photography appears on its pages.

Karl E. Lutze

Other books by the author:

To Mend the Broken
   (Concordia Publishing House, 1966)

Forgive our Forgettings, Lord
   (Concordia Publishing House, 1972; 2nd printing 1980)

Of Walls and Doors — a Procession through My Life
   (Fairway Press, 2001)

Awakening to Equality —
      a Young White Pastor at the Dawn of Civil Rights
   (University of Missouri Press, Spring 2006)

For more information contact Orchard House,
                                    P.O. Box 469
                                    Valparaiso, Indiana 46383

Table of Contents

VII. BRIEF LIFE

VIII. UNFOLDING OF LIFE

Foreword

Though the terrified child might cry her prayer all in an instant, the prayers we plan to pray require time and an easy contemplation. They must become experience. They name and initiate the genuine experience of the presence of our Lord. And so they reward the time and times together, because we go forth in the renewal of our relationship with God.

In this volume, Karl Lutze's lingering prayers give words to those who yearn such contemplation. They make the mind alert and the heart tender to the various parts of our days, to the multitudinous needs of our souls, to the feelings both good and bad in them we love, to human experience, to God's gifts, to the times of our lives.

Read them one a day. Read them first out loud and then in the mystery of your silences. Fill their details with the details of your own particular life. Name those most touched by the prayer which you are praying and making your own. See what you say. And if you are willing, rock your upper body as though the prayer had music your inner ear is hearing — and so, engage the whole of you.

These prayers, these "I" soliloquies awaiting your voice, will reward you.

Walt Wangerin, Jr.

Introduction

Late in the summer of 1969, some two dozen executive officers of the larger Lutheran church bodies, as well as national leaders of Lutheran Lay organizations, gathered on the campus of Augustana College in Sioux Falls, South Dakota. they had come to hear almost fifty American Indians speak out on their experiences with Lutheran churches through the years, and also to share their ideas about how Lutherans might achieve a wholesome relationship with - and better serve - the larger Native American community.

I was to provide an opening devotion. When I stepped to the podium I told them such an important meeting deserved solemn reflection. I also acknowledged that they were an unusually diverse group of Lutherans, to be sure, but also Roman Catholics, Baptists, Episcopalians, Unitarians, Pentecostals, Presbyterians, people who practiced Native American religion, some who had no ties with any churches or religious denominations at all.

I explained my feelings of awkward discomfort, imposing on others any prayer I would speak, and yet I did not want to back away from speaking my thoughts at this moment.

So I suggested that each reflect on what we would be about in these hours - in whatever way one would choose. I would speak a soliloquy with my God. I would do so aloud and, should any wish to eavesdrop on this conversation, they were surely invited to do so.

Several people approached me later to express appreciation for what I had done, and for my words. They urged me to share such soliloquies again at the opening and close of all the days we would be together. I did, and have been using that form of reflective mediation in meetings and workshops ever since. Some of these formed the content of my book *Forgive Our Forgettings, Lord,* in 1972 and again in 1980.

. . . a Lot on my Mind, Lord contains more such soliloquies. Each is an expression of personal contemplation, a personal prayer. You now are invited to listen in and to share in these thoughts.

I suggest - whether whispered to oneself or spoken aloud in a group - that the reading be slow, measured, and deliberate.

For All Seasons, All Places

Right Now, Lord!

God, my friend,
I have so much on my mind –
      so much to talk about,
      so much to say,
      so many questions to ask –
            I hardly know where to start.

And then you whisper into my ear,
                into my heart,
      your word for me at this hour:

         "Be still –
         And know that I am God!

    Be still.

    Be still,

Be still – hush now – and know that I am God."

God of darkest nights,
God of brightest days,

God of deep forests,
God of desert sands,

God of expansive oceans,
God of trickling streams,

God of green pastures,
God of oil wells,

God of noisy factories,
God of happy playgrounds,

God of heavy traffic,
God of lonely paths,

God of soaring airplanes,
God of slowly rolling wheelchairs,

God of the bugles of battlefields,
God of mothers' soft lullabies,

God of celebrations,
God of cemeteries,

God of lonely cells,
God of crowded stadiums,

God of scenes of tragedy,
God of medical centers,

God of yesterdays and yesteryears,
God of all tomorrows,

how brash and arrogant of me
to beg an audience with you,
in midst of all your caring
for all of your creation –
as if you have not already known
what's in my heart
and on my mind.

Yet you yourself have issued me
a standing invitation
to return again
and again
and again.

So here I am again;
no need for many words.

Keep me remembering
    you are God –
        my loving, saving God.

    And I am yours
        and all is well.

        AMEN

The New Day

Still Alive – No Surprise

Another day –
    I should be surprised, but I'm not.
        Every morning there are some
        who never did survive the night –
            accident,
            violence,
            heart attacks,
            or "natural causes" –
        for many, last night *was* the last night.
    But I am here – alive!

    And even though, when I was small,
    I learned to pray
        "If I should die before I wake,"
        I've found myself
        quite used to death not coming
        and I'm not surprised at all
            at waking up alive.

Each night as I prepare to sleep
    I have every expectation
    that tomorrow, too, I'll be among the living –
that's what has happened every morning of my life so far.

I am not asking, Lord, that you would cause me
        to be gloomily awaiting my last hour;

    instead, I pray that I may highly prize
        each day you give,
        each day you let me live,
            as precious hours entrusted to my care;
            I want to use them well.

        And as I contemplate,
          anticipate,

and wonderingly await
what lies ahead of me as
time unfolds,

give me the wisdom
not to overlook
the hours of this new day I now begin –
nor let those hours
slip away between my fingers.

Let my ears be open to the sounds of laughter –
mine and others' too –
that in those sounds
I hear a melody of praise to you,
the God who makes hearts glad;

And let my ears be open to the sounds of labor –
and let me hear
the roaring of monstrous trucks,
the scratching of pencils,
the thumping of great machines,
the humming of computers,
as both the efforts and the toil of
those who generate the sounds;

And let my ears be open to the sounds of sorrow –
let me hear
the gentle weeping,
the frantic sobbing,
the pounding of an anxious heart,
and low and tired voices,
hoarse in their calling out
for solace and for friends.

And let my ears be open to the sounds of nature –
the soft refreshing breezes,
the call of a bird,
and the bark of a dog –

that in those sounds
I may discern your creation
and your caring
all around me.

In this day that you have given to me, Lord,
let me see smiles and sparkling eyes
and happy strides –

and help me see
eyes moist with tears;

and help me see the sober look,
the wrinkled brow,
the slower step,
the lips that cannot form a smile.

And help me, Lord, to see myself –
receiver of your grace
and your forgiving love,

inextricably bound to you –
spared, protected, sheltered –
yet sent –
sent into this day
to bring your love
to all I meet;

that when this day comes to its close,
I might recall
the many ways you've been with me today

and with great joy give thanks to you
for giving me this day
and helping me to use it well.

AMEN

Morning's Newness

A new day, God.
        Perhaps not altogether new –
        not new for me in the same way
                that it is new for the puzzled chick
                    bursting from its shell
                    on unsure legs, looking about
                    to see light for the first time,
                        and a new world;
                to try out its new and untried voice
                with outrageously unmusical shrillness;

                to hear for the first time the gentle,
                    reassuring clucking of its mother hen;
                to taste for the first time a tiny sipping
                    of cool and refreshing water –

      no such a day is hardly mine,
              for much about today is old –
                    not really new at all.

The very bed in which I lay
    last night before I slept
      is that in which I found myself today when I awoke;
      I've seen the skies before;
      I've seen the grass and trees;
      and in my mirror is the face
            I've seen a thousand times.

And when I looked to see the time,
        the time piece showed me numbers
            I could recognize – I've seen them countless times.

And when I looked to see the time,
    the time piece showed me numbers
        I could recognize – I've seen them countless times.

The water I splashed on my face
    I've felt before.

This getting up to meet the day
    is nothing new to me at all.
The clothes I choose to wear this day,
    the food I eat,
        the people whom I see,
            have all become familiar.
    And my responsibilities,
        and chores to do,
        the letters to write,
        the unfinished assignments and commitments,
        and the bills to pay –
        and unsolved problems and nagging aches or pain –
    I'm somewhat quick to say about this day
        and all it brings
            "It's nothing new!"

And yet in Holy Scriptures
you persist in telling me,
"Behold, I make all things new!"

    And that's good news.
    But those same words invite me to *"Behold."* –
    to open up my eyes,
        to look around,
        take notice, and
        to comprehend.

Your *making new* gives promise
    that for me there are new possibilities,
        new ways of looking at past events;
        new ways of doing things in familiar places;
        new ways of responding to people I have known
                before.

You, in Christ's cross,
    bestow forgiveness on me for the failings of my
                        yesterdays;
You, in Christ's cross,
    give me new visions of your love –
        your love for me;

You, in Christ's cross,
    present me with a new assessment of the many people in
        your world –
                those far away and even those in distant lands
                whom I have never met or known;
                    the rich, the starving;
                    the brutal and the gentle;
                    the conniving and the pure in heart;
                    the agile and the feeble.
    You show them all to me as people
            whom you've loved and whom you love
                as dearly
                and as much
                as you love me.

You, in Christ's cross, O God,
        show me new ways of seeing
        people all around me –
            some whom I barely recognize,
            as well as faces that are dear to me;
            and some whose presence brings me little joy at all.

And there are faces that I do not ever get to see –
        faces hidden behind prison walls;
        faces shielded from my vision by a thousand other
            walls
                in hospitals
                and nursing homes
                and flimsy little shacks
                and lofty penthouses,
                and tenements;

and deep carpeted, oak walled offices;
faces covered with beards – or shawls
belonging to people who have no walls or
roofs –
no place at all to call their homes.

That cross calls on me – and gives me strength –
to view all these and countless more
as people you desire
to be your very family.

You send me out this day
to look at them
and live with them
as brothers and as sisters to me.

And, God, I know that brothers and sisters
often do not love each other well –
their envy
and their jealousy,
their arrogance
and superiority
can prompt behavior that can
cause a parent grief –

And, surely, ways in which *I* have treated
or neglected others –
these my sisters and my brothers –
must have grieved and deeply disappointed you –

and yet you give me forgiveness,
a new day
with all my past behind me –
and give me words to say again – anew:

Creator, Savior, holy parent, Lord,

Create in me a clean heart, O God,
And renew a right spirit within me!
Restore to me the joy of your salvation

as you lead me into this new day.

AMEN

Alarm Clocks and Church Bells

Alarm clocks and church bells
    and bugle calls and crowing roosters
        woke your people this morning, Lord.

And some awoke to sirens and flashing red lights and the smell of
smoke
      and some to persistent pounding on the door,
        not knowing who was on the other side.

And some were roused by screaming children
      and others by some sharp and frightening pain.

And there were people, Lord, who stayed awake all night,
      who twisted and turned
        and could not sleep at all –
and others sat in waiting -
      struggling to stay awake –
        eyes open – but they waited anxiously,
          torn wretchedly between
        their hoping
          and their fearing
            yet the worst –
        worried mothers,
        frightened refugees,
        those awaiting surgery,
        or even execution.

And my night, Lord?
You were at my side
and at the side of all.

No hair unnoticed,
every sparrow watched –
and flowers in a million fields
and parks and gardens
or in painted pots
or florist shops –
You decked them out, O Lord,
more regally than Solomon
in all his royal robes.

You, caring Lord, you were with me –
and with my loved ones
and with all your people;
you were there –

and you have brought me to this day –
your gift to me –
not just another day –
but a day with you;

and thus a day in which the worst hours of my yesterdays
are all behind me
and forgiven –
because of you.

But yet this is a day that builds on all the good things of my
yesterdays –
        such good gifts you have given me:
        the loved ones who attended
                all my tender years of growing;
        the beauties and the freshness of your breathtaking
                creation;
        the warmth and strong encouragement
                that come from friends;
        the learning and experiences I've had;

        my Baptism;
        and your Bread and Wine;

        the gracious promises you give – and keep!

On these I build this day you give me, Lord.

Open my eyes and ears and heart to all its goodnesses
      that I may say with courage and strong faith
        "This is the day the Lord has made;
           I will be glad in it,"

    that once again when it is ended
        I might bow my head and say
            that I have walked with God today –
                and it was good.

AMEN

Thank You for Sparrows

It's another day Lord;
        however, I admit I've not yet fully felt
           the freshness and excitement
           mornings are supposed to bring.

I don't know whether it's more sleep I need
        or just some time to rid myself of
        unrelenting pressures;

or whether some problem I thought I could manage
        still remains unresolved,
           bothering me
           and weighting heavier
                than I even realize –
    or none of the above.

I only know that for the moment I feel quite alone,
        and I'm not even sure that friends
        are what I need right now.

I'm not quite sure what I would say,
        where I would even start –
           I know I need to think things out,
           but thoughts get jumbled and confused –
        and then I look outside
           and I see sparrows.

I'm grateful, Lord, that you give sparrows.
        Country or city – there are sparrows.
        Summer, winter – there are sparrows.
        Rain or sunshine – always sparrows.

Sparrows,
                    hardly prettiest of birds,
                    brazenly enduring busy traffic
                    and the hazards of icy storms
                              or drenching rains
                              or scorching sun –

          no striking plumage like the cardinal,
                    no elegant menu like the waxwing,
                              who insists on berries,
                    or the goldfinch,
                              who prefers black thistle seed.

The sparrow seems resigned to humble ways,
          seems quite content and satisfied
                    to settle for a crust of bread
                              or table scraps –
                    to be ignored, unwanted,
                              called "nuisance" and "pest."

People erect elaborate houses for the martins
          and build tiny ones for wrens,
          but who has ever built a sparrow house?

                    The sparrow,
          resented and disdained,
          you single out, O Lord,
                    for me to focus on this day.

Though there be millions of these tiny birds,
          you tell me not a one can drop in flight
                    but that you know.
          And speaking of providing them a nest,
                    you tell us that your altar, Lord,
                              will give birds like these shelter
                                        and a home.

At times when I feel of such little worth,
    you show me sparrows to tell me
        that you care for them
        and that you rank me of much greater worth –
        and surely, I know this.

I know the message of an infant's birth in Bethlehem
    and how, when grown,
        he gave himself to caring for the lonely ones
        and troubled folk
    and how in his own hours of near despair,
        when facing torture of the cross,
        he did not swerve
        from giving up his life for all –
        and I am counted in that *all!*

He rose again, I know, that I might be a child of yours
    and, more than a surviving sparrow,
        I'm one whom he has chosen
        for his very own.

Come to me this day, O Lord,
    as you have come in earlier days
        to weary prophets and psalmists,
        fumbling apostles
        and countless   dispirited Christians.
Breathe in me again your spirit;
point me from the cross
    to the day that lies ahead
        with all its tasks and opportunities
    and go with me in it –
        just as you have promised.

AMEN

At Day's Close

Each Minute a Gift

I usually have things I want to do each day, Lord.
Sometimes my plans are careful,
detailed, and quite precise –
I set my clock,
arrange my chores,
and know just where I must be going,
where I'll stop,
and just how long I will be staying.

And when the day comes to its end
and I've achieved all the things that I had planned,
I have a freeing feeling of accomplishment –
a day well spent.

But, then, there are the times when evening comes
and I look back upon the day;
I see how much that I had hoped to do
remains undone –

The countless, unexpected interruptions
by loved ones
and strangers
and telephones
and mechanical failures
and diversions so temptingly pleasant
and accidents
and demands of other people's agendas
that claim priority over mine –
all those – and more – conspire to make a
shamble of my plans.

And when the day comes to its end,
I'm left with feelings of frustration.

And I can only hope tomorrow will be free of all
the obstacles that blocked my way today
and I'll get done the list of things I want to do.

And there are days when plans I've made
seem hardly significant at all.

Sometimes I even say, "Today I'll take it easy"
or set aside the whole day for myself –
for entertainment or amusement –
to be with friends –
or by myself.

And such refreshment can be gratifying, Lord,
a gift from You.

And some days when I set such easy. pleasant goals,
I fail to realize even those aims:
in spite of all intentions,
I let myself become enmeshed in work
that should have been ignored,
or else I waste the time allotted for refreshment
and miss out on the revitalizing
you intend for me.

Lord, as I await tomorrow,
my prayer to you
does not merely seek your help
so I might be decisive in ordering my life
and persistent in implementing my own plans;

I ask instead that *you* would give me grace
to learn what *you* want me to do *for you*
in that new day that lies ahead.

Help me, my Lord, to see each minute
that a million clocks tick off
as gift from you.

And help me to see all the happenings
unfolding before me
as opportunities to do your will.

And help me in each person that I meet
to see an invitation as from you
to love that one as warmly and forgivingly
as you have welcomed me.

And help me in my thoughts find opportunities
to recall and think upon your Son
and all he's done for me

So that I can truly say
I want to live that brand new day for you
determined not to turn aside
or let myself be swerved from serving you.

And when the day is past
and shadows fall upon your world,
give me joy to look behind to see
how richly you have blessed what I have done –
and give me grace to grasp the full forgiveness
you bestow so generously on me
putting aside,
as far as east is from the west,
that which I've mis-done
as well as that which may remain
neglected and undone,

and give me strength to live the days that lie
ahead –
to make plans and set my mind,
surrendering both my hands and all of me
to do the work that you want me to do –

help me remember I am yours,
that you regard me
as your friend
and member of your family.

O, walk beside me, Lord,
as I live for you who died for me
and live in me!

And now, my gracious Lord,
put all of this days' happenings far behind me
and give me quiet rest
in your forgiving, strong embrace.

AMEN

Unlock the Doors

Out there in the night, Lord,
    there is so much uncertainty;
    people walking quickly,
        glancing over their shoulders,
        fearing that someone may be following;
    people in their cars,
        gripping the steering wheels
        until their arms ache,
        straining to see the road
            beyond the rain or fog
            or blinding headlights
                until their eyes burn.

Out there in the night, Lord,
there is so much uncertainty:
    sirens pierce the quiet, signaling emergency;
    panic-stricken people waiting for the fire truck;
    dazed survivors of an accident waiting for the
                    ambulance.

Out there, Lord,
    frightened people lock themselves away
        from howling storms
        or those who might do violence;
    and others are afraid of dangers close at hand,
        dangers from those at home,
            deranged or vicious,
            or maddened by alcohol or drugs.
    And yet others, frightened by their own thoughts,
        worry over loved ones;
        agonize, anticipating their tomorrows;
    others pace the floor in sleeplessness,
            torn apart by nagging guilt.

Lord, your disciples were frightened people
    the night the soldiers came,
        when swords flashed
        and you were led away;
            and, panicking, they ran
            and locked themselves away.

But in your own way,
    in your own time,
    then you came
        into their night of despair,
        into their loneliness and fear,
        into their locked and bolted room.

You raised your wounded hand
    and spoke the gracious word, "Peace."

And that hand said it all:
"I have tasted loneliness and terror,
 I have tasted abuse and pain,
 I have tasted bitterness and doubt.
 I have tasted these
        and taken them into myself
        and I have returned to give you life –
                            life in fullness."

Lord, recall this scene to me –
        even when my night is not frightening,
            that I may be aware of those
                whose nights are filled
                with bitterness and fear.

Help me respond to the charge you give:
        "I send you as the Father has sent me."
    that I might bring to people as I can
        your loving care,
        your word of peace.

Then what I say and what I do and what I am
    is in your stead, and
   in your name, and
   in your power, and
   in your love.

AMEN

Assessing the Day Ending

End of the day, God.
You've seen many such;
    for a while you numbered them
    and at the end of each you said "it was good".

There've been so many days since then
    and you stopped placing numbers on them.
    After ever so many of those days
    you must surely have said "it was *less* than good".

Those first six days were really good
because those days were marked by your creating –
    creating first a place
        where you would bring forth life
            and nourish it
            and sustain it
            and be multiplying it over and over again.

The days that followed,
    the days that I assess as bad
  are days when blood's been spilled,
      that day when parents screamed
              and wept their   bitter tears
            because brother had murdered brother;

      that day when Herod's swordsmen slashed the
      children in their cribs;

      that day when men rose up with poisoned hate
      and in religious arrogance
      smote dead your Son;

      that day they crushed the skull of Stephen
      with their heavy stones.

All such mean deeds assaulting your creation
　　on any given day
　　make that day bad.
And yet you in your loving, caring way persist
　　　　in countering the bad to fashion good!

For every day you bring forth life –

　　- flowers with their seeds,
　　- the tall stalks of grain,
　　- and calves in nursing at their mothers' side,
　　- and newborn infants on their mothers' breasts;

　　- recovery for those subdued by illness
　　-and healing for the wounded limbs.

　　you still bring life –
　　　　you rescue lives,
　　　　　you restore life,
　　　　　　you enrich life,
　　You prolong life.

　　and when you bring experiences
　　　　like these into my day
　　　　I, too, am moved to say "And it was good!"

But when I learn how people hurt –
　　how some are left to die because they have no food;
　　how some are left impoverished
　　　　because of callousness or greed
　　　　　of some who would be rich;

and when I hear how some are left neglected
who need medicine
and healing
and shelter
and companionship
by those who "pass by
on the other side – "

and when I recall the many folk
whose lives are damaged,
shortened, or destroyed
on any day –

then I lament the happenings of that day and say,
"And it was less than good."

Dear God –

I've done my share
of hurting people
with my words

and sometimes with my silence

and sometimes by my turning from the very ones
who need what, in caring love,
I might have shared with them –

And this day is another when I've loved less well
than you would have me love.

This day is another
when I've forgotten
and neglected persons who desperately needed
the friend I might have been to them.

And when I count the ways I've disappointed them
                    and disappointed you
                    and disappointed me,
          I tend to look upon the day and say
          "and it was less than good."

But in these closing hours –
     as you once promised –
your Holy Spirit "calls to remembrance"
          what the Christ has communicated
                    to me, both by his words
                    and by his life:
          that you love me,
          that you forgive me,
          that you claim me as your very own,
          that you will stay with me this night,
                    and every day and night,
          that you will refresh me
                    and strengthen me for the morrow's
                    assignment:
          that I be busying myself with
               loving and enriching
                    the lives of others.

     This is the life, creating, re-creating Lord: –
          to have you living with me
                    and in me.

     All this you've done for me again this day –
          and it was good!

          AMEN

Workers-in-the-night

Tonight, Lord,
    while I sit
        quietly reflecting on the day
        that's ended now
    and readying myself
    for my night's sleep,

    I remember those for whom
        the hours of darkness
        are their time for work –

The waitress calling out her order to the cook,
    who winces at the cloud of greasy smoke
    that rises from the grill –

The truckers who
    as if on signal
leave their booths and stools
each going to that monstrous carrier,
    climbing high into the driver's seat
    dwarfed in the great machine
    and causing its awesome engines
        to roar in the darkness.
    One by one
    they slowly roll into the highway lanes,
        their lights making for them
        a pathway into the black night;
      and though the other trucks ride near,
        each driver is alone again,
    eyes trained to follow
        the ribbon of white that marks the road –

one hand fastened tightly to the wheel,
    the other fumbling for the steaming coffee cup
    while late night music fills the cab;

they face the blinding lights ahead
and thoughts of loved ones flood their minds –
and countless other thoughts –
and as the miles and hours pass,
those monstrous tires slapping on the road
compete against the Diesel engine's roar.

And there are nurses and their aides tonight
in rest homes
and in hospitals
for whom the hours can pass so slowly and so silently
as they patrol the darkened corridors,
but who stand ready
for the bells and lights that call
for help –
who quickly run to be with those
who wake disturbed
by dreams or sudden pains
or nagging fears –

and officers this night,
dispatched to accidents,
who deal with broken glass
and twisted steel
and people who are sobbing –

the men and women who must go
to tell a mother or a wife
about a loved one's death –

The list goes on –
night watchmen,
those people at the fire stations
ready to respond to each alarm;

the engineer who guides those endless lines
of cars that clatter down the rails
across the countryside;

airplane personnel whose tiny lights up high
appear so very much like distant stars;

and sailors and soldiers;

and those who in the night make hallways
and offices, cafeterias, stores, classrooms,
restrooms and streets clean once more
for those who start *their* days with
mornings;

as well as those
prepared to deal with crippling emergencies
when storms blow in
and wires come down
who in the foulest weather –
sleet or snow or flood – are there
to make things right once more –

And mothers –
and fathers – who awake
to tend their fevered children
or a dear one up-in-age
whose last hours are nearing –

I forget all these so easily.

And in the light of day when I meet up with these
who work at night,
I seldom realize
the roles they fill
while I and others slumber,
oblivious of these who toil
into the early morning hours.

You, Lord, have often heard me ask
for your protecting hand
to hold me fast
as my eyes closed in sleep.

Tonight I ask again for your continued care for me;

but more,
keep watching over all your workers-in-the-night.

Forgive me
for the times when I – in thoughtlessness –
have made their nights more difficult;

and give me grace to be
a thoughtful, kind, and caring friend
to all of them –

as you would have me be,

remembering
and following the Christ,
your son, our Lord,
who's loved us well,
enabling us
to love all those

whom he has loved
for whom he died,
for whom he lives,
and whom he loves both day and night.

AMEN

People All Around Me

Sometimes, Lord, I choose to be alone,
     away from jingling telephones
     and radio and television noise
     and voices that call for me to listen and respond –
        I welcome then the quiet
        that allows me time to think
         and to reflect
           and contemplate
        the hours and days that lie ahead.

But only *some*times, Lord –
     for I would agonize,
        were solitude *imposed*, not by my choice;
        were I deprived of company
        day after day
        for days that stretched to months
        and months to years.

But you have filled so many days of mine with people, Lord.
  With some I've lingered
  and I know their faces well:
     faces that were kind and caring;
     faces that, without a word,
        spoke understanding and concern;
     faces that welcomed and made me feel at home;
     faces that made me laugh
       and gave me courage
       and made me feel strong.

And there were always other people who were there
     but whom I hardly saw at all:

waitresses who take orders,
bring the food, refill the cups;
and I've not noticed who they are
or how they look
or what they say and do;
churchgoers in the pews ahead,
whose dark or light or curled
or bald tops
I can gaze at,
but whose faces I don't see;

children crowded on the playground whom I see
as one collective noise
instead of each, distinct and separate,
a bud awaiting its full flower;

flight attendants, soldiers, nurses, or police
whose identities are lost
in the uniforms and rituals of duty.

How much I miss, Lord,
when I fail to see each one of these
as persons you have made
and loved and care for –
as persons you still care for –
when I forget that they are gifts from you to me.

In my passing by, unnoticing,
I miss what you intend for me;
for each of them has something, Lord,
from you to me –
perhaps a word that's kind,
perhaps a smile,
perhaps a downcast look or frown
that nudges me to see my neighbor's need.

And in my passing by, unnoticing,
how often I have missed the opportunity to love –
to speak the word that would encourage one
whose spirit droops,

to direct one who's confused,

to offer – to the friendless – company,

Your world – so big, O Lord!
Your people – Oh, so many, Lord!

And now as night falls
and my eyelids grow heavy
I am near to closing my eyes on all of this!

I praise you, God, who never slumbers, never sleeps,
that your eye stays – stays fixed on me
and looks on me compassionately
and protectingly
throughout the night,
throughout my life –
and on those dear to me, my loved ones
and my friends,
the old ones and the new;
and on those too
from whom my own eyes
turned away,
that all of them might share with me this joy
of being in your presence.

And one thing more, Lord –
      when my eyes open with the morn,
                   (be it here with you
                    or there with you)
    give me new vision
    to see each person that I meet
           as one who's loved by you
                at cost of blood
                  and pain
                  and death,
    that I may value each of them as you do;
      and help me, forgiven and enabled by your spirit,
    to be friend to them
    and faithful unto you!

    AMEN

Discipleship

Let Me Walk with Those Twelve

I wonder, Lord, just how those Twelve you chose
     reacted to your startling invitation
     when you enlisted them to follow you.

The record does not tell us
     that the ones who fished
         first straightened out their nets
            and hung them up to dry
               or put their boats in dry dock
               or sold the fish
                  they'd caught.

Nor do the Scriptures tell us
     that the tax collector who joined your ranks
         first filled out the proper forms
            and made his final entries in the books
            before he took to following his Lord.

Whatever once may well have been the pulls upon their lives
     no longer loomed important for these men;
as if they'd dropped some great and heavy chains behind,
     they left their busy, cluttered lives to follow you.

            Day and night for three full years
               they walked and ate
                  and slept and learned
                  while at your side.

          And nothing else
          and no one else
             meant more to them
             than being in your company.

While there with you
     those Twelve began to glimpse
your Father's pure intent in sending you
     to visit on this earth.

And when, with loving hand,
     you touched the aching limbs to heal
and gently spoke your gracious and forgiving
     words to troubled folk,
those followers of yours
could see how singlemindedly
     and lovingly
you walked the heavy journey to the cross
     for them
     for all of us.

And once again, arisen and ascended,
     you still were with them, Lord
and helped them see themselves
     unfettered by this world's constraints,
their lives no longer cluttered
by all the things that once had seemed so all-important
to each one of them.

First stumbling and faint of heart,
     those faithful apostolic men matured
     and, by your grace,
braved every obstacle and death itself
with singleminded dedication
     to the task of serving you.

What models, Lord, for me!

But I can hardly be like them
        for all around me are the daily confrontations
            which beset me and distract me,
                demanding my attention and my time
                and sapping strength and energy,
                insisting that your call for me to serve
                        can wait.

Forgive me, Lord, for times when I've forgotten you
                or have regarded *your* concerns
                        as less important than my own;
        and give me now new insights

so that what I regard as distractions *from* you
        might become opportunities for service *to* you;

let the disrupting noises little children make
                alert me to become your instrument
                        of care and love
                to these, your precious ones,

            and help me be aware that underneath
            the harsh, demanding ways
                    of family
                    or friends
                or even casual acquaintances

        may lie a desperate need
                for compassionate understanding
                that may lead to useful change
                    in them,
                    in me;

            and help me recognize that troubled lives
            of people everywhere
            are opportunities for me to bring
                    your comfort
                    and your healing.

For you, Lord Christ, confronted all of this and more
    when you were here upon this earth –
    and I so wish to follow you!

Lord, more and more, help me to set priorities in order
    that nothing clutter or obscure the path
                    I take in following you
                    in selfless, faithful service.

And when the path is rough or brings me pain,
    help me remember YOU,
                    familiar with such paths,
                    are walking with me
                    all the way.

                    AMEN

Preoccupied with My Troubles

It almost seems presumptuous, Lord,
    for me to ask your undivided attention now,
    as if my concerns would be most important –
       while in great cathedrals
            and hospital halls,
            in cemeteries
            and maternity wards,
            in darkened prison cells
            and sun rooms of retirement homes,
    troubled voices are whispering petitions
        far more urgent than my own,
    begging for an audience with you.

And yet you invite me to come again and again.

No matter how petty and small my requests may be,
when weighted against such heavy burdens others bear,
    you promise not only to notice, but to listen –
                     to hear me out.

       My failure to respond to faces and voices
           all around me   that call out
               for compassion and help,
       my preoccupation with myself
           and the things that make me happy
               or that trouble me,
       my fretting about my future –

All these loom so large to me –
    and yet they seldom match the agonies that others feel –
       lives bent by death, made empty by loss,
          pained by disease or accident,
            rendered hopeless by defeat,
             made desolate by loneliness,
               isolation, or imprisonment.

I find it awesome that you do not turn away from such –
        there are so many!
                and *their* fears and terrors so intense!
Yet you keep inviting <u>me</u> to **call** in every trouble –
        you promise neither to ignore me
        nor to ridicule my coming as absurd
        nor cast me from your presence, Lord.

You tell me I'm important,
        dear, and precious to you.

And I recall
        a stable with a manger;
            a dark hill with three crosses;
                a garden with a huge stone rolled aside –
        there he is – for me –
                your Son,
                    my Brother,
                        my Savior,
                            my Friend.

And in remembering him,
        all things I ask of you find answers –
            perspective for my life,
                forgiveness for my sin,
                    direction for the days ahead
                        support for every step I take,
        for you are present at my side –
            before, behind,
                beneath, above,
                    around me
                        and within me.
And so, in being close to you,
        I also have drawn close enough
to note those others who keep calling out to you.

O help me, Lord, that I no longer be preoccupied
                with all these troubles of my own.

Keep me aware of those whose lives are torn
    by every kind of anguish,
        whose hearts are broken,
        shoulders bent,
          and spirits crushed.
And help me, in your name and with your love,
    endeavor to respond
    to all who in their need cry out for rescue and for help –
        to those whose frightened cries
          are loud and shrill,
        to those whose voices have grown hoarse
          with their persistent calling,
        to those who deep in desperation now at last
          in weariness have fallen silent.

O give me both the strength and the compassion
    to bring to such the love that you intend for them
        with words of encouragement
        with selfless gifts and deeds of love,
    sharing the good things you have given me –
        forgiveness,
        welcome,
        hope,
        and company on life's journey,
    in Jesus Christ, my Lord, my Friend,
        and theirs.

AMEN

When I Don't Feel Brave

Lord,
>   when I don't feel like being brave anymore,
>   when courage slides from me
>   and I tremble inside,

>   when all I find within me
>   is weakness
>   and inadequacy,

>   help me recall that there were others too
>   who, when they found their strength was gone
>   and every hope as well –
>   when fearing for their very lives –

>   still found the words
>   to say: "Lord, save us – we perish!"

And reassure me, faithful friend,
>   and raise your loving, powerful hand
>   and say once more
>   to wind and wave and storms
>   and frightening futures:

>   "Peace, be still!"

>   AMEN

You are Always Here

Amid the rush of busy chores –
        demanding tasks –
        looming deadlines –

suddenly we find refreshments –
        like oases –
        like cooling water –
        like delicate fragrance –
        of a desert flower –
            a smiling face –
            an understanding glance –
            a quiet word that says
                "I care" –
              those special moments
              when a piece of work is finished –
              and the inner voice says,
                "Well done!"

At those times –
when it seems our work will never end –
I say my prayer of thanks
        for each such resting place,
        each encouragement.

Still –
        there are thorns
            and sharp stones along the way
              that make me wince and cringe –
              and sometimes cry out –
                a troubled spirit –
                a broken heart –
                a bodily pain –

and as children do,
I long for
a Father's strong and gentle hand
to heal and hold me fast.

And lovingly to every child who calls you say,
    "I am not deaf –
        yes, I can hear your call.
    I am not blind –
        yes, I can see your need.
    I surround you
        with my love
        and with my faithful promise to be near,
    and I surround you
        with loved ones in whom I dwell –
        as they speak and touch and embrace you
        they give to you my love."

Hear Lord,
and every day remind me
that, though I wake or sleep –
        remember or forget,
you are awake –
and you remember me –
you are still at hand
        close,
        strong,
        loving.

And give me wisdom to say my word of thanks.

AMEN

Safe in Peril

God, whom I so often call "My Savior,"
    I realize that when I call you that,
    I acknowledge that you *saved* me.
And that means I am safe.

I am reminded by preachings
    and teachings
    and crosses on top of churches
    and by your Holy Supper
that I am "saved."

      The hymns I sing,
      the psalms I hear,
      the Scriptures that I read
      assure me I indeed am "saved."

And though I'm thus assured
    and reassured
    that I am saved,
why are there times I feel that I'm not SAFE?

Grave tragedies still come to human life
    from swift and overwhelming floods,
    from fiercely devastating, whirling wind –
      those hurricanes,
      tornadoes,
      the tidal waves
      and all the storms at sea;
    from fires raging through the brush
    and flaming timbers
      crashing to the ground;
    from cars that fold at impact   with each other,
    reduced to splintered glass
    and shredded steel;
    from savage bullets and from bloody knives.

These tragedies, from which I want to shield my mind and close
        my eyes, are all around –
                the headlines of their stories leap at me;
                the gory details bring burning to my eyes;
                the commentators' voices pierce my hearing –
                                        and my heart.
        And I should like to wash my mind of all of it
                        and wipe it from my memory.

Yet, like the steady pounding on a drum,
                the sordid stories keep on happening
                and keep on being told.

        In such a world
                it's hardly easy to feel safe.

        And there are tragedies more subtle –
                no less tragic –
                        the loneliness that comes with loss of friends –
                        when loved ones leave,
                        when people we have trusted turn on us
                                        and fail to be true friends,
                        when dear ones die,
                        when health begins to fail,
                        when cancer strikes,
                                or injury or some disease
                                        deprives a person of full use
                                        of skills that used to be
                                        so valuable and strong.

And some through drought have seen
                their farm lands waste away;
        while others, robbed of livelihood –
                by reverses in their business,
                dismissal from their jobs,
                or loss of their possessions;
        and there are those who see their loved ones die
                a little every day

for want of proper food and care.
God, who declares me saved,
I want so very much
to be SAFE from all such agonies.

Indeed, you invite me
and all the sons and daughters
you have called your own
to come like frightened chicks
to find both warmth and safety
under your protecting wings –

But you have more than safety for me, God. I know.
As lovingly as gentle, clucking mother hen,
you claim the role of mother eagle for yourself.
While you've prepared a place for me
to nest in safety
and to grow,
you, like the eagle, often make our nest uncomfortable –
you stir our nest;
into our lives come troubling confrontations
like sticks that poke and prick us;
you bring us to the times
when we can test the strength
you give
so we can fly – free and unafraid.

And when I find my strength is weak
and tend to plummet toward the earth,
you soar beneath me, bearing me
upon your strong and trusty wings,
and patiently you teach and nurture me
to make me strong and confident,
equipped to fly. –

The flight you send me on is not away from you;
   you promise ever to be near,
      directing and sustaining me;
Nor do you want me flying far away
      from other children of your brood.

Help me to have strong wings that I may fly
    with eyes as sharply focused as your own,
   that I may see the many challenges
     that all your young ones face –
     the ones whose wings are not yet strong –
         nor injured yet by life's harsh storms –
     the ones who still are inexperienced in flight,
    those not quite ready yet,
       those unprepared to face the risks
         of new and bruising blasts;
      the ones who cower, terrified –
   that I might listen for their panicked cries,
      assuring them I stand at their side,
        supportively, as a reliable friend..

And help me help the timid and the fearful learn to fly –
    to show by my example
      and my caring words
        and patient willingness to listen
  how they themselves may come to be mature,
    caring for others of the flock
    and in full flight and strength –
      with us – be following you.

AMEN

My Dearest Friend

God, whose very own I am,
   who watches when I wake or sleep,
   who knows my every step,
     my every thought,
     my every word before it
       even moves across my lips –

who's there with me
     wherever I may go –
     persistently, unceasingly,
       unfailingly,

how easily this wonder slips my mind,
especially when I find myself
     in places that are strange to me;
     and sometimes too with people
       whom I do not know,
with people who do not know me
     or even seem to care
     whether I am there or not.

In loneliness I long for a familiar face,
   a caring voice,
   for sights and sounds
     that might just make me feel at home
      and comfortable.

The clocks and watches
   all become intolerably slow;
     and yet it seems that only time
     will be a friend
     and change all this
     and bring me once again
     to the company of loved ones
     and places that are home to me.

But still I know
such yearning and such longing
can only rarely be fulfilled,
for places change
and people change
and sometimes people move away.
And some, of course, have breathed their last.
And some have taken on new ways
and are so different now –
absorbed in other lives
and other interests than those
we shared so long ago.

But you change not.
Your constant company
your watchful and protecting care
your love that will not let me go –
all these remain with me.

You, dearest Friend, you choose
to break into my solitude,
to waken in my memory
your gracious words that welcome me
into your warm embrace,
assuring me that all my negligence
and little faith,
and preoccupation with my own concerns,
you generously put aside in your great mercy.

And when I taste your bread and wine
and find renewal for my life
as I receive you in your Supper
and call to mind that wondrous Friday
when you yourself were so alone,
you, Lord, remind me still that you know lonesomeness
and understand your people
when we feel alone.

Fill every lonely corner of my heart and mind
    with such rememberings
    that I may find what once seemed loneliness
      a blessed moment
      for enjoying you,
          my best and truest Friend,
          my Savior and my loving Lord,
          who's ever near to me.

    AMEN

Concern for Maturity

O God, whose child I am,
    I've spent most of my life
    trying to be less and less a child,

    wanting to be regarded
    and respected as mature –
    as being capable of making wise decisions,

        no longer needing others to make choices for me,
        no longer leaning on others,
        no longer dependent and subordinate,
        no longer having to answer to others
                for my personal life;

But through the years I've come to treasure
    quiet moments –
    like this one, Lord –

when I can talk with you
    and honestly acknowledge
        how unready and underprepared I really am
            to face the fears
                and problems
                    and responsibilities so nagging and persistent
            in my life –

the ones still left from yesterdays
                and yesteryears
      and those that spring anew
            like weeds and mushrooms –
        to take the place of those
      I thought I'd finally dealt with.

So now I welcome conversation with you my Parent God, and,
even more, your gentle invitation to be "child" of yours,
    admitting all my limitations
    and inadequacies,
            my smallness and my tiredness,
            and my need for you,
    and my need for your courage,
                your forgiveness and your strength,
                your presence,
                and your wisdom.

And let me, in child-like faith
    and in child-like honesty,
    and in child-like joy,
        appreciate the lovingly surprising responses
        that you have for me in every need.

Then, Lord, with you here at my side,
    let me perceive the child in people all about me,
    to discover – underneath their calm and sure exteriors –
        the insecurity and doubtings that they hide,
            to understand the loneliness that
            must be theirs
                if they have none whom they can trust
                to tell of their unsureness –
                their need for guidance and for help.

And help me gently to communicate to them
    perhaps not even with my words –
    that I desire to be a friend to them,
        though I'm not always strong,
        that I may gladly share with them the friendship
        that you've given me.

And one more thing, O Lord –
Give me the grace to be especially patient
 with those young ones, God,
 who desperately try
  to keep from showing
  that they're really young
  and in their very efforts to be grown-up and mature
  reveal how unsurefooted yet they truly are.

Keep me from laughing,
  from being condescending,
  from treating them as inferiors;
 keep me from distancing them from me,
   disdaining them,
   dismissing them as immature
    and having no real worth,
 lest I myself behave as immaturely
 as my first parents' child who blurted out in self defense
 so long ago: "Am I keeper of my brother (or my sister)?"

Let me see each one of these young people then
 as members of your family – and mine –
 for whom you have as great a love
  as that you have for me,
   that I myself prove worthy of the call
    that you've extended me to be your child,
    and share that love with them –
    and all your children everywhere.

AMEN

God's Gifts

Mealtime, Lord – Again !

Mealtime, Lord – again!

Morning, noon, and evening
    and often in between
    some things may not get done,
    some hardly get begun –
        but eating, even on the run,
        I seem to squeeze into my busiest of days!

    I'm glad that when I was small
        my parents took the time
        to help me fold my hands
        and say the "Come, Lord" prayer. –

        Eating is, of course, for all of us
        the sign of our dependency on you.

We cannot live –
    and therefore could not even think of doing work
        without the nourishment you give
        so freely in our daily life.

And more than this that's spread before me here,
    you give me nourishment unspeakable
        each time I taste the bread
        and sip the wine
    with which you give your very self to me,
        to celebrate the Holy Supper time,
    the familyhood of which you make me part –
        a foretaste of the feast to come!

And if that were the only meal,
it would be quite enough!
But no! You give us even more –
again, again, again –
our *daily* bread!

So cause me to remember now
before I lift a single morsel to my lips –
YOU, Lord –
you supply all my needs;
oh, open wide my eyes
to see your purpose
in this nourishment:

that you intend for me
to be alive, alert, enabled
for your service, Lord,
to share your bounties
with all those who hunger
for food,
for friends,
for shelter,
for company,
for direction and
perspective –
all those who hunger, Lord,
for YOU
and all your goodness.

And now, to you, who never yet has left my side
(and even now are here with me!)
I say with grateful heart:

Welcome, Lord Jesus, precious Guest,
and let these gifts to me be blest.

AMEN

The Days are God's

Lord God,

When shifting layers of rock and clay
first burst the crust of earth,
and towering mountains thundered into being –

    YOU WERE THERE !

When nations rose in pride and power,
           and crumbled once again,
             only to be replaced
by younger and still more strident nations –

    YOU WERE THERE !

You've seen the ships your creatures built
      to venture out into the seas;
      and then in later years, the ships that flew;
      and now, the ones that soar through space.

And when we say "Time passes on," we err –
      for time is *Yours* and it is *we* who pass.

Lord,
      you have seen – and watched;
          our childhood
          and our growing
          and our learning
          and acquiring skills and insights;

and you have blessed us richly with your gifts:
the loved ones who have nourished us;
the friends who played and learned
and worked and grew with us;
our teachers, our experiences,
our health – all these and more.

Forgive us Lord, for thoughtlessness – and thanklessness –

and lift our eyes
to see the doors you open wide before us now,

that with courage and wisdom –
and excited by your presence –

we may move into all
of the tomorrows that you give to us,

eager to serve you
and your world
and your people everywhere
with confidence,
selflessness,
and integrity,

in the spirit and style of Jesus, in whose name we pray,

AMEN

Special Days

My Holy Holidays

Lord, I remember Christmases –
    the Christmases
        when I was very small
        and I could hardly wait
    for all the night would bring:
        the presents spread beneath the tree
        and on the table good things to eat;

    and Christmases
        when finally we sang the carols
        and spoke the lines we had rehearsed –

    the Christmases when I was grown –

        and watching others
        open gifts that I had brought
        meant more than presents given me;

        when the music – and the candles
        and the lights
        reflected in a child's wide eyes –
            meant even more to me.

Yes, I remember many Christmases, my Lord.

And I remember Easters too –
    the sunrise visit to the church,
    the pungent fragrance of the lilies,
    the people dressed for spring,
    and tinted eggs and jelly beans.

Yes, I remember Easters. And Thanksgivings too,
    with family crowded close around the table,
    the table spread with food –
    the turkey and the dressing – all the trimmings there!

Lord, I remember
  Christmases – Easters – Thanksgivings –
    I remember,
    but with a heaviness –
    not caused by sadness for things past;
        a heaviness that comes.
            because with all my celebratings
        I often give so little
        thought and thanks to you;
                the setting and the frills –
                the incidentals –
                become the centerpiece,
        while you and what you've done for me
            I remember so briefly
            and take for granted.

And even now I list
        the gifts, the jelly beans and turkey –
            the things that once delighted me,
            and in this hour delight me still.
Even now
        I've failed to name
            the reason and the purpose
                in all those celebratings.

Awaken my dull senses, Lord –
        call to my mind a manger
            with the smell of straw,
            the heavy stomping of the restless cattle there.

        Call to mind –
                so that I see again
                the Son of God
                given to me in the Infant,
                the God for me to hold close,
                the Savior who holds me close.

And nudge me to recall
   the early morning hour
   when grass was moist with dew
   and small flowers opened fresh
   and birds made their first song of the day.

 Call to my mind that morning's empty tomb
  so that I turn and see
   the Son of God with arms outstretched to me,
   the hands spread wide and open,
   showing the cruel marks of love –
    so that I fall before you with deep joy
    and say, "My Lord and my God!"

Let my days, dear Lord,
recite your gracious deeds
and let my nights repeat the wonders of your love,
   that in my celebrating
   all year round
   I bow my head and say,

    "O give thanks to the Lord
     for he is good;
     his mercy endures
     and endures and endures."

    AMEN

The People of Christmas Eve

The crowded stores,
   the burdened postal workers,
      the brightly decorated houses,
         the special choral concerts,
            the busy airports –
all these, and more, combine to tell me
   how much this season
   touches so many lives, o Lord.

And, though surely much of all the seasonal activity
      has little to do with remembering
         the Bethlehem event,
    there still will be vast numbers
     who find their way to worship
     in a thousand places
         all over the world.

And still others,
    who do not find their way
        into the candle lighted churches,
   will keep the festival
   in family circles
   or in lonely settings –
         in hospitals,
         and prison cells,
         or in their tiny living quarters.

Lord, though I may see a portion of those crowds,
I'm likely more to concentrate my thoughts on me
    and people close to me
     this night.

Tonight, I pray,
give me a vision of three scenes:

THE FIRST:

    a glimpse of little boys and girls,
    who in Christmas costume
       find their place among the shepherds.
      In hushed excitedness they discover
       their Christmas happiness
        in the Baby;
       and they sing to him –
            this is their gift to him.
      this is their gift to him.

THE SECOND SCENE:

    here are the more mature –
    like Gospel writers,
      Luke and Matthew
      who, alive with memories
        of the first Christmas
        (and past Christmases as well,)
    are occupied with making
    subsequent Christmases memorable.

THE THIRD SCENE:

    moves me beyond the children
    and those in the in-between years
      to people in their later days –
       the folks resembling
        Simeon and Anna.
  These are the ones
      whose eyesight may be dimmed,
       yet now in clear perspective
        have captured and hold fast
        the view of what this holy night
         is all about,
      and what *IMMANUEL* means to them:
       not only *God with us,*
      but soon we shall be *there with God.*

With these three scenes in mind, Lord,
on this holy night I pray,

give me the grace to be as unself-conscious,
                as unembarrassed
                as uninhibited
                as tiny children,
        that I may in spirit
        kneel at your manger
        and sing carols to you
                with raucous joy,
                as that night the angels did.

Open my mind, Lord,
to recall the beauties of Christmases past:
        the candles and the colored lights,
        the gifts and the music – and the dear ones
                softly singing Silent Night with me.

And open, Lord, my eyes
to look about me to see
        and to remember
        those whose hearts this night are heavy
        and whose tears cloud their vision
                and almost smother their hopes,
that I might help them
        find a chamber in their hearts for you,
                and discover your enormous love anew.

And best, Lord,
　　give me the maturity and the perspective of the wise
　　　　to make room for you
　　　　and welcome you
　　　　into *my* own heart and life,
　　so that, reflecting
　　　　on the purpose for your coming,
　　　　I may – with more than empty words –
　　　　　　but with genuine kindness
　　　　　　and caring,
　　　　　convey your forgiveness
　　　　　　and your love to all,

　　　O dearest Jesus, Holy Child . . .

　　　　　AMEN

My Familiar Walls – Good Friday Thoughts

I find comfort, Lord, inside my own familiar walls.

I call these walls familiar –
and things inside almost become like "family" to me:
 the chair,
 the bed,
 the table,
 the little things
  that make me feel I'm "home" –
   framed pictures,
   snapshots,
   books,
   and letters –
    remembrances of people
    who've been here inside these walls;
   they're family folk –
    my family of friends.

     And I recall the voices,
     laughter, whispers, music –
      the fragrance of fresh flowers,
      and aroma of a meal,
      the scent of Christmas branches
        and of candles.

These walls I call familiar
 shield out the blowing snow
  and drenching rain,
   the icy sleet and
    frightening storms
     and darkness
     and noise
    and strangers and dangers.

Lord, I know well how stifling it can be
       to stay within these walls and be confined.
How good it is to feel fresh breezes on my face,
       to hear the birds,
       to smell the flowers,
        to see the sunsets
           and so I venture out.

And, to be sure,
       outside the walls
       are beer cans, broken bottles and debris
           and choking clouds that trail the trucks
           and hang above the cities –

and there are
       impatient horns,
       sharp tongues
       and violent tempers
       and tensions
       and tears
       and pain
       and fear –

           I really care for none of this,
           and I can hardly wait until
           I'm comfortable and safe again
           inside my own familiar walls.

So I am not much different from eleven frightened men
    who years ago found refuge in familiar walls
    and locked themselves from all
    the horrors that were striking close.

They spared themselves
                the brutal taunts of angry mobs,
                the screams and sobbing
                        of the faithful few who would
                not leave the chilling scene
                        of wailing and death.

    You, Christ, were there – outside the walls,
    showing care for those who could not care less,
            those sporting beneath your bleeding feet.

    You, Christ, were there – outside the walls,
            speaking hope for one who'd wasted his life.

    You, Christ, were there – outside the walls,
            giving comfort to the aging woman,
            giving friendship and family
                        to the lonely single one.

    You, Christ, were there – outside the walls,
            offering forgiveness and new life
                for everyone of every age.

Lord, keep me from sitting in my safe familiar walls,
    locking myself from the world out there
            which you so loved
            and into which you've pointed me.

Come gently, Lord, into my life again
        as you came to those frightened men;
                raise for me your nail-pierced hand
                and say again "Fear not"

that I may venture out for you into the world
outside the walls I've built,

                finding there the ones
                to whom you send me,

that I might bring them
                your forgiveness,
                your compassion,
                your welcome,
                and your love.

And when I am reluctant,
        when I hesitate in fear,
                then call to my remembering
                your promise to go with me as I go.

                        AMEN

Contemplating Labor Day

In this busy world of yours,
you orchestrate a symphony of labor with your gifts, O Lord:
>the farmer who mounts his heavy-engined tractor
>>to turn the soil and plant the seed;
>the logger who fells the great timbers;
>the secretary, typing with swift fingers;
>the surgeon who wields the scalpel;
>the craftsman who turns the whirling lathe;
>the musician who teaches the pupil to sing;
>the driver who glides a massive tank truck
>>with its volatile load through lanes of
>speeding traffic;
>the engineer who designs a bridge
>>to span the great river;
>the therapist who helps once-broken legs
>>to walk again;
>the judge who listens to the witnesses
>>and speaks the verdict
>>>to the anxious court;
>the chemist who varies the formula
>>ever so slightly a thousand times
>>to find the one that will effect a cure;
>the firefighter who scales the burning wall
>>to save a screaming child;
>the chef who prepares the food
>>for those who crowd his tables;

all of these you use – and countless more –
>>these are the workers of your world.

And some begin each day of work with prayer on their lips,
>while others are unmindful of your presence
>>or your caring.

And where do I fit into all of this?

I hardly can persuade myself that what I do
    is really so important
    in the vast and complex scheme
    that you've designed for your creation, Lord.
Nonetheless, unworthy though I feel
    and insignificant,
    I know you have a place for me;

    your Scriptures picture you as our Head,
        and we by grace are members of your holy body.
    So none of us who claim such status in that body
        dare ever say
        to even lowliest of members:
        "I have no need of you."

So help me, Lord, to seek my place
    and see my task
    and firmly grasp
    and fully comprehend my life
    with your perspective.

And help me, Lord, to do my work
    with joy
    while saying thank you from my heart.

Help me, Lord, to see the young ones all around
    eager to find their place –
        impatient with the waiting,
            yet still unready
            for the work you have for them to do.

Help me seize each opportunity
    to help them build their skills
    and hone their minds
    that they may be prepared
    and equal to the tasks that will be given them by you.

Creator Lord,
     help your people see how we have soured
        and spoiled
        and neglected
        your creation –
        and your creatures.

Redeemer Lord, you came to the people of the world
     to bring order out of chaos,
        peace out of conflict,
          life out of death.
Help me, to be a faithful follower of yours,
           whom you've redeemed – at great cost.
    Enlist me, equip me, and enable me
       to be an eager agent of your reconciling work.

Spirit Lord,
     breathe freshness into me,
        that, cleansed and forgiven,
        I may live my life faithfully,
        manifesting in all I think or say or do,
        the love with which
           I've first been loved;
        and give me joy
          in my pursuing such commitment,

AMEN

Brief Life

At a Loved One's Death

Good and ever present Lord,

So often I forget you always are at hand,
and in my failure to remember,
   it is easy to regard you as absent,
   as not here at all,
       as though everything that goes on in my day
       happens quite without you present.

In your brief stay upon the earth
   you frequently would visit with your friends in Bethany,
     with Lazarus and both his sisters,
       with Martha and with Mary too.

You loved that family much.

And when that brother died,
you shared the news with your disciples,
     telling them, "Lazarus is sleeping."

Then lest they misunderstood, you told them plainly.
   "Lazarus is dead."
 And you were deeply moved
       and you wept.

Today my heart is heavy too,
as one I've loved has died.

And I can understand why Martha, long ago, lamented,
   "If you'd been here, Lord,
    you could have preserved his life!"

O Lord, I would not wish for any who have died to resume
whatever heavy burdens they were carrying.
Nor would I wish they be deprived of the new life
that you have given them.

But, oh! the emptiness and loneliness I feel
without that dear one near!

Good Lord, remind me of your reliable promise
that you'll be with me always,
not as occasional visitor, but constant companion,
who has chosen to make my heart
to be the place you are at home.

And while I slowly traverse in these hours
the awesome clouded valley of the shadows of death,
remind me
that you are at my side
and that you once walked this valley – alone
for me, and for all – the departed too – and,
at that death walk's end, rose to assure me
that you have prepared a place for us
at your great homecoming banquet.

AMEN.

Death Comes before I'm Ready

Lord, you often let death come to people
        before I'm ready.
It's not my intent to question your wisdom –
        but with most of those you take to be with you
        who've meant – and mean – so much to me,
                I'm not yet finished!

        And there are those now gone
        with whom I'd not yet started –

        I'm speaking of those who died
        whom I never met –

                some whose death occurred even before my birth
                and some who died more recently
                but whom I never got to know.

I speak of those whose lives
have made a contribution to my own –
        and I so wish I knew
        all they have done to bring
        enrichment to my life –

I long to know much more of those
        whose gentle hands first washed
        and blanketed my tiny frame
        when I was born.

Whose arms were those that comforted
        my infant sobs when I awoke
        and parents were not there?
        Whose voice sang hymns and hummed the lullabies?

Who were the ones who taught me games
    and how to read
    and sing
    and say my little prayers?

And I have questions, Lord, to ask of people
    I have known
    and are no longer here to hear them
      or give answer –

I long to know so much of those
    who've gone before –

    about *their* childhood –

        how they toiled, how they laughed,
        how they agonized with conscience
            or with pain;

how they risked, or how they failed
           when paralyzed by fear;
    how they loved and celebrated,
    how *they* worshipped,
    how *they* faced lonely hours
      and disappointments;
    how *they* grieved and how *they* dealt with death.
        What hidden strengths were theirs?
        What needs and yearnings?
        What angered – what delighted them?

And what would they have wished for me –
    what heritage –
        if ever they could dream of days like these
        or such a one as I?

Such thoughts have special pain for me
　　　when I remember those
　　　whom I have known
　　　and lost more recently –

The times I spent with them were often wasted hours –
　　　hours that passed far too quickly by –
　　　often in awkward pointless conversation;
　　　and now I think of countless questions
　　　that remain unasked –
　　　　　　unanswered.

Three lessons, Lord, you have for me
　　　in this awakening:

First – help me to revere the memory of loved ones
　　　who have gone before,
　　　the ones who made my being here a possibility at all –

　　　the precious family memories;
　　　　　the love I found even among the struggles
　　　　　that go with the shaping of a family and home;
　　　　　the opening of my mind
　　　　　　　to see where you fit in it all.

And second – help me to note the shortness of our days,
　　　that I may treasure every hour
　　　　that you have given me to spend
　　　with strangers, friends and loved ones –
　　　　　knowing they are pilgrims too;
　　　　and help me learn to know
　　　　　their beauties
　　　　　and their strengths,
　　　　　their weaknesses and needs,

　　　　　that I myself may grow in wisdom –
　　　　　　　and in faith.

And third – help me use well the time that I have left to live
and so to count each day I live
as gift from you, my Lord,
and use each day in wisdom,
to serve you as I seek to bring
healing,
hope,
and welcome
to all of these – before they leave,
before I leave.

AMEN

The Unfolding of Life

The Nurseries

Lord, you've said that little ones are precious to you
   and you speak blessings on all such
      who treat them lovingly –

   It really isn't hard to love them
      when they're well-behaved,
      considerate, helpful,
      and obedient

      or slumbering
      or cooing softly in their cribs

      or frightened
      and trusting me.

But there are times when children seem impossible –
      the tiny ones
      who cry and cry and cry
         and cannot tell us why
         and nothing we supply
         can bring the storming to an end –

      and when that happens,
         when we need it least
         (in a church service!)
      or when that screaming
             drowns out other voices
             that we want or need to hear

      or wakes us
             when it still is very dark
             and desperately we want
             and need to sleep

or when we are confined
in train or bus or plane or car
with nowhere to escape.

And there are other times
when rather than just loud
these young ones turn hostile
and rude;
they defy our every effort
to be kind and patient
and understanding
and reassuring.

Their impudence
and stubbornness
and disrespect of others
prompt thoughts of anger
and vindictiveness in me
which I abhor –
the feelings that begin
to gnaw on me
make me ashamed.

I need to turn to you, Lord, for perspective –
you've been there Lord; that I know,

yourself a child,
so good, so pure,
you surely must have been resented
by the children
who likely heard their parents say,
"And why can't you be more like Jesus?"

You must have known and felt the cruel taunts
and ruthlessness
that children can so sharply launch at others.

Help me to see that younger ones
    so often have quite wretched models
        to observe and imitate –
            styles of life in which they grow –
                when older folk themselves behave as immaturely
                and as selfishly as spoiled children.

Help me, Lord, not to regard children –
        because of their small stature
            and limited development –
        as creatures less than persons;

Help me regard them, Lord, while still so young
        as *your* persons.

            A rose plant is a rose
                before it flowers,

            it is no less a rose before it blooms;

            and there can be no flower of late summer
                without the early greening of its spring.

So help me then to lift the infant gently,
            to touch it in those tender growing years with care,
that I may not forget the unfolding
        of the fully flowered person
            you intended – and intend –
                in your creating every one of them.

And help me to recall that all dear people
        whom I love most
                and most respect
were once themselves small children –

who in their childhood
had their own moments
        of discomfort
        and disappointment
        and likely weren't good company.

And I, of course, was one of those
        whose pouted lips
        and angry tears
    exposed me as unlovable –

and yet adults –
        my parents and my teachers
    and my neighbors
    and a host of others too
    – and especially you –
                forgave and offered second chances
                        again
                        and again
                        and again.

So help me, Lord, to draw a long deep breath –
    and fill me with your loving Spirit

        so that in patience
            and understanding
                and wisdom
                    and vision
                        and hope
                            and love
I may meet and welcome all young ones
        you bring into my presence
with the love with which I have been loved –
        by others
        and by you.

AMEN

The Awesome Role of Parenting

I find it almost frightening, God,
   when someone leaves a baby in my care –
      so fragile
      and so precious –
      so utterly helpless and dependent.
   How can I know, if crying would begin –
         and grow to screaming –
   how can I know just what it is that hurts or frightens?

Even more, what can I do – what <u>must </u>I do!

Parents too must sense the staggering responsibility
   that is theirs,
   (only multiplied a thousand times)
   when *they* take on the role of caring for young children
   and do so
   not for one brief hour or so
   but for each day the child is given
      for growing into ripe maturity.
Each day – and every night! –
   <u>nights</u> when sudden crying
      wakens everyone within the house;
    when tiny ones are hot with burning fever
   or when they waken, terrified by frightening dreams;

  and <u>days</u> when they come
       whimpering through the kitchen door,
    utterly and totally defeated
    because some unkind – or thoughtless –
     word or action crushed their tender feelings.

And parents know a tearing of their own hearts
    when first the infant's left with some else
        (as well as pages of instructions
        and phone numbers
        and all manner of precautionary warnings!)

And then at length there comes the day
    when little ones go off to school –
        perhaps a half day,
        possibly all day –
and never does a single day last quite as long
        as that first day of separation.

The realistic parent knows that this is only the beginning –
    the first of many flyings from the nest;
        the venturing away
                to stretch and exercise the wings
    But little wings
        and growing wings
                are never really strong as they will be,
                    as they MUST be.

    And, as they grow,
            in headiness
                they can indeed fly perilously high
        and, determining to make it by themselves
        can swoop low down to dangerous depths,
        sometimes testing,
                    risking far beyond wise limits;
            and sometimes,
                lacking confidence
                    that they are viewed by others
                        as mature, responsible,
                    timidly, they seek refuge
                        in some corner,
                    hoping to avoid a challenge
                        which they feel
                        they'd surely fail.

Parents want so much to be there, standing by;
and yet they cannot (nor do the wise ones really want to!)
    manifest distrust
    or keep their young ones tied –
    and fettered! – to themselves.
They want to help them to grow *up*
    and yet not to grow *wild*;
They want to love,
    yet not to pamper them.

O you, who bids us call you Father,
    O Father of all children
    and of all parents
    and of me too –

Lord, help me see my role and calling:
    a member of your family –
      that I may gladly stand with parents everywhere
        as they accept the task
        of helping shape young lives.

Help them – and me – to see each child
    and every growing person
    as objects of their parents' caring –

and help me be supportive to all parents –
(they are my sisters and my brothers too!)
      as they spend time and energy
      and effort and their very selves
        in caring for and guiding these young ones
          who desperately want to –
          and, no less, truly need to –
          move on out into your world
            with full maturity.

Forgive me, then, resentment that I may feel for parents
      whom I regard as less than wise,
      whose parenting I would disparage.

Forgive my shortness and impatience
        with the young ones who behave in ways
        so different from the way I would prefer they did;

Forgive me, God,
        for having less love for these
            than *you* have for them –
            and for me –

and help me to stand before your wretched
        and most holy cross
            to hear once more your gracious words
        "Father, forgive them!"

and even more, help me
        to capture the intent of what you said
            to John and to your mother there –
            "Be family with each other;"

that I may take those words into my life
        and, strengthened by your powerful love,
        be family with all parents
        and their young ones everywhere.

AMEN

Commitment to the Young Ones

Lord God, whom Jesus addressed as "Father"
and to whom he looked for care
and for support,
you guarded and protected him
from infancy to manhood
through loving parents
and specially dispatched angels,
your messengers of care –

Hear me as I pray, as I reflect
upon your children everywhere –
the tiny ones and toddlers
as well as those grown larger
than their parents;
for all of them I pray:
the hungry and the sickly;
those healthy, those robust;
the bright, the slow;
the gifted and the well-to-do
and those impaired;
the poor and disadvantaged too;

for those who have already stumbled
and those who contemplate
the compromising of integrity –
as well as those still innocent –

and help my prayer to be commitment
rather than mere words;
that I commit myself to caring
for all children – who indeed are yours –
with patience and understanding,
with listening ears
and words, both firm and kind,
with generous heart and open arms,

as I endeavor to stand strong and helpful
    with parents everywhere,
    and with those who work with youth –
        the caregivers,
        the teachers,
        the coaches,
        the counselors,
        and all who serve in schools
          and colleges and universities,

that I recall with grateful heart the love with which I myself
    through all my years of learning and growing
      have been so generously blessed by you,

that I in selfless love for them may thus be serving you.

AMEN

On a Thousand Playgrounds

Lord,
    when I'm with people who have made it past the time
        when they were young,
    I find myself forgetting those who have not yet arrived
        at full maturity –
            But sometimes when proud fathers
                or proud grandmothers
            produce their wallets with the myriad photos
                of their progeny,
                    all beautifully groomed
                    and holding still
                    – almost in agony –
                    while waiting for the camera's flash
                    so they could once again return
                    to all the vigorous and bursting vitality
                      and reality in which
                      they find themselves.

At such times I'm reminded of those tender lives
      you've placed among us in the world
            and – oh – you've given us so many.

If I possessed your omnivision
and could see them all,
    I'd catch them on a thousand playgrounds,
        in gymnasiums
           and in parks
        pumping high on straining swings,
        pushing up and down on teeter-totters,
        splashing in tiny pools
            or diving into little ponds
              or streaking though the lanes
                in rhythmic contest,

leaping up for rebounds,
    dribbling, passing,
      pitching, catching,
        chasing batted balls,
  jumping rope and racing –
     flying kites, rowing boats,
      dancing
        singing
          keeping rhythm with their feet
            while pounding sounds come roaring
             through their earphones
               as they ride their bikes
               or fly by on their skates –

And some are standing 'round on corners
  and some are tinkering with antiquated cars
    and others make their souped-up engines roar
      or squeal their tires in sudden stops –
and some are glued to TV screens
  and others are absorbed in electronic games
    and some go wandering aimlessly through alleys
      while others sit in quietness on lonely hillsides
    and others seek the crowds.
Some are curling up with novels or with magazines,
  some up so late into the night
    in desperate attempt to rescue a semester's grade
    with reading or writing
      in libraries
      or in some sheltered study nook –

some hitching rides,
  some drinking,
    some partying,
      some scared of their tomorrows,
        some very cocky, very sure –

some using gifts that they've been given,
    lovingly
    with gratitude
    and faithfulness –
some wasting these and having no idea
    of what they want to do or be;

some hungry,
    some huddled in the darkness
        frightened
            because they've been abandoned
            or because a violent parent hovers near;
and some confused
    because their home is torn
        by tension and brutality –
and some because of war or other tragedy
    too soon become like men and women
        before they ever could be simply children –
and all of these and more
    you tell me now to love.

How awesome, Lord,
    and how impossible –

and yet you give me partners to go with me in all this –
    parents and foster folks,
      Scout troop leaders,
        social workers,
          counselors and youth leaders,
        pastors and coaches,
         doctors and nurses,
          big brothers,
           big sisters,
             uncles and aunts,
             Sunday School teachers
         and all kinds of teachers –

and most of all, Lord,
  you give me promises,
     the same kind of promises
     that have attended me
        from my mother's arms
        – and father's too –
and brought me in spite of my wanderings
               in spite of my protestings,
               in spite of my stubbornness,
             in spite of my selfishness,
             in spite of my weaknesses,
             in spite of my doubtings –
brought me to this hour and this place.

I have seen how you keep the promises you make,
     and I've found you to be trustworthy,
       patient,
          forgiving,
             and giving me strength –
             just as you have promised.

     And you promise to go with me.

Be at my side then,
    strong,
      to help me join supportively
      with all who see
      and care about
        those young ones of yours all around,
           everywhere – in every corner of every land,
             of every race and language,
        those young ones who so very much need
          your understanding – your love;

that I may, with these allies you have given me, reach out –
    generously,
        with understanding,
        compassion,
        and with love
            to younger ones,
         remembering your words –
"Let the young ones come…for of such is the
Kingdom!"

Even so, Lord, Thy Kingdom come.

AMEN